C000270860

Feeding on God

*If we will not learn to eat
the only food that the
universe grows—the only
food that any possible
universe ever can grow—
then we must starve
eternally.*

C.S. Lewis, The Problem of Pain,
HarperCollins

*'For my flesh is food indeed,
and my blood is drink indeed.
He who eats my flesh and
drinks my blood abides in me,
and I in him.'*

John 6:55–56 (RSV)

FEEDING ON GOD

Shelagh Brown

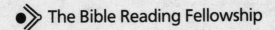
The Bible Reading Fellowship

Text copyright © Shelagh Brown 1995
Illustrations copyright © Sister Teresa Margaret CHN 1995

The author asserts the moral right to be
identified as the author of this work.

Published by
The Bible Reading Fellowship
Peter's Way, Sandy Lane West
Oxford OX4 5HG
ISBN 0 7459 2971 0
Albatross Books Pty Ltd
PO Box 320, Sutherland
NSW 2232, Australia
ISBN 0 7324 0937 3

First edition 1995
10 9 8 7 6 5 4 3 2 1 0

Acknowledgments
Unless otherwise stated, scripture is taken from The Holy
Bible, New International Version (NIV) copyright © 1973,
1978, 1984 by International Bible Society. Used by
permission.

The *Revised Standard Version* of the Bible, copyright ©
1946, 1952, 1971 by the Division of Christian Education of
the National Council of the Churches of Christ in the USA.

The *New Revised Standard Version* of the Bible, copyright
© 1989 by the Division of Christian Education of the
National Council of the Churches of Christ in the USA.

Illustration on page 36 reproduced by permission of
the Bursar, Coventry Cathedral.

A catalogue record for this book is available
from the British Library

Printed and bound in Great Britain
by Cox and Wyman Ltd, Reading

CONTENTS

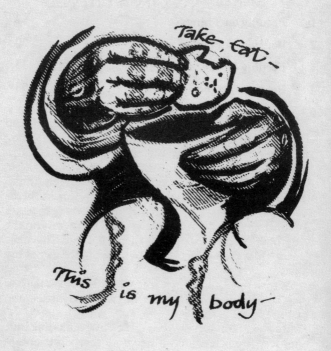

I

FEEDING ON THINGS

Just over an hour ago I was in church, eating the bread and drinking the wine of communion. Now I am sitting in my garden under a big umbrella, eating warm croissants with butter and drinking freshly made coffee.

Whatever we eat and drink is astonishingly transformed into us. My croissants won't appear as themselves tomorrow morning, after the digestive processes of the human body have been at work on them. But the cells of my body will be fed by them, and I shall have the energy to wake up tomorrow to live another day of my life.

When we feed on something what happens is that we take it into ourselves. It enters into us, nourishes us, and becomes part of us.

But as I am sitting here under my pink and blue umbrella I am feeding on far more than croissants—which anyway I finished after I had written the first paragraph of this chapter, and then scraped all the last flaky crumbs on to the last bit of butter and left the plate totally clean. It was the croissants and coffee that gave me the idea of where to start—but as I was sitting in church listening to the words of the communion service I was reflecting on the whole idea of feeding, because I was praying about writing this book, and wondering how best to begin.

At the eucharist, too, there was much more entering into me and becoming part of me than the bread and the wine. I was hearing the words of the service, the Bible readings and the sermon. The sunlight was streaming in through the stained glass windows, and I could feel the warmth of it on my head and shoulders. When Richard Thomson, the vicar, prayed, he thanked God for the sunshine and the warmth and the light of it, and he asked that each one of us might know the great warmth of the love of God in our hearts.

Now, as I sit in my garden, there is a great feast of things all around me, and it is as if I am drinking them all in to myself and being fed and nourished by them. The smell of the new-cut grass, which I mowed yesterday, and the cool feel of it under my bare feet. The warmth of the June sun on my right arm and shoulder— getting so warm that I am just about to move further round under my umbrella. All the different greens of the grass and the trees against the clear, tender blue of the sky. And the creamy white umbrella heads of the hogweed growing high above the grass in the field.

My tame blackbird is hopping round on the grass— with his tail feathers starting to grow again after a cat or a magpie pulled them out. Big, baby starlings are squawking to be fed by their parents—though they are larger now than the parent birds and look quite capable of feeding themselves.

In my herb patch there is the blue-green of the sage and the bright, shiny green leaves of the bay tree. The feathery foliage of the fennel reaches up to the lower branches of the apple tree, and the spikes of the new lavender are beginning to grow up.

I can hear the birds singing, and the sound of a horsebox driving slowly up our bumpy road. The horses who live next door to me are stamping and snorting contentedly in their stables as they pull at their bags of hay, and a single-engine plane is flying overhead.

I can smell the honeysuckle—one of the sweetest and headiest smells in the world—and taste my delicious coffee, continental roast. I had it in a bluey-green pottery mug to go with the blues and greens of a Portmerion plate—and on the plate there is a painting of a *Hyacanthus Orientalis*, or Eastern Hyacinth, with four exquisite blue butterflies painted on it as well. A moment ago a real-life butterfly flew past. Just an ordinary cabbage white. But awesomely beautiful. And a house fly sitting on my table is cleaning its front legs by rubbing them together.

Up in the field there is a pond, with toads and frogs, newts and fishes—and brilliantly coloured damselflies and dragonflies darting and hovering over the surface and sometimes being snapped at and eaten by the fish. In the winter mornings a heron stands motionless by the side of the pond, looking into the dark water for the stirring of something to feed on. Then he plunges—and a frog or a fish becomes the heron's breakfast.

A few yards away there is a blackberry bush. I didn't plant it—it just grew there. I suppose that one day a bird dropped a blackberry out of its beak by mistake, and it fell into the earth, and the tiny little seeds started to grow. Now it covers half the fence—and is covered with masses of pale pink flowers. Later in the summer the flowers will have been transformed into big, juicy blackberries—and the birds will eat them and so shall I. I shall make some of them into bramble jelly and others into delicious blackberry and apple pies—and my friends and I will eat them with cream when they come to supper.

But my blackberry bush gives me much more than

bramble jelly and pies. For me it's a way of feeding on God, and a symbol of my sort of spirituality.

Some years ago I came across Oswald Chambers' wonderful book *My Utmost for His Highest*, and because of it I prayed this prayer. 'Lord, whatever it costs you, and whatever it costs me, I want to be the best I can be for you.'

I wasn't thinking about the cost to God-in-Christ of his death on the cross. I knew about that—and I knew that I was loved and forgiven. What I was praying about was my spiritual growth to Christian maturity—and I wanted God to persist with me to make me the best I could be.

So far as the cost to me went, I wasn't volunteering myself as a candidate for an illness. I was thinking about the denials of my self that would be like small crucifixions, as I set myself to say for the rest of my life, 'Not my will but yours be done.' As God took me up on my prayer (he always does on that sort of praying—so be careful!) I discovered that the disappointments in my life also formed part of the pattern—and I realized for myself the truth that St Paul knew and wrote about: 'we know that in all things God works for the good of those who love him' (Romans 8:28).

The other thing that I definitely didn't have in mind when I prayed that prayer was that I should become one of the world's great saints like St Teresa of Avila or St Francis of Assisi. For me they were great oak trees of saints. I had something much more ordinary in mind, and what I thought was that I would like to be the best blackberry bush I could possibly be for God. Rooted in the safety of the earth—and in the love of God. Growing upwards, in the warmth of the sun, the rain and the wind, the frost and the snow—all the things that would happen to me in my life.

The birds make their nest in the blackberry bush in

my garden—like the sparrows used to in the temple of God—and they find a home there. The birds and human beings eat the fruit—sweet and juicy and delicious. Blackberry bushes are very ordinary—very common—and they grow in any soil. They also have prickles (certainly like me—and possibly like you), and for me that makes being a blackberry bush for God a real possibility!

Moses saw an ordinary bush in the wilderness once, burning with fire but not burnt up. So he went to take a closer look at it—and God told him to take off his shoes, because the place he was standing on was holy ground. My blackberry bush is like that for me—and like Elizabeth Barrett Browning's poem.

> *Earth's crammed with heaven,*
> *And every common bush afire with God;*
> *But only he who sees takes off his shoes,*
> *The rest sit round it and pluck blackberries.*

Elizabeth Barrett Browning, Aurora Leigh

But some of us who pick them and eat them can see the glory too—and when we open our eyes the whole of creation can be a way through to God and a way of feeding on God.

My blackberry bush grows in the rich brown earth that I have added lots of manure to, from the stables next door. The blackberry loves it and so do the roses. Good rich soil—full of the goodness that they need to feed on—rooted and grounded in richness.

For our lives to grow really well we must have our roots in the right soil. We've got to be rooted and grounded in love: from our mothers and our fathers and our friends—and from God. If we've never had enough human loving then the love of God can make it

The WHOLE EARTH is FULL of his glory

Isaiah 6³

up to us. We can be transplanted into it, so that we can feed on it and be nourished by it—and in the next chapter we shall look at how we feed on people through our personal relationships.

But for now we're thinking about feeding on things—and Jesus told us to look at the creation and think about what it taught us about God.

> 'Look at the birds of the air; they do not sow or reap or store away in barns, and yet your heavenly Father feeds them. Are you not much more valuable than they? Who of you by worrying can add a single hour to his life?
>
> 'And why do you worry about clothes? See how the lilies of the field grow. They do not labour or spin. Yet I tell you that not even Solomon in all his splendour was dressed like one of these. If that is how God clothes the grass of the field, which is here today and tomorrow is thrown into the fire, will he not much more clothe you, O you of little faith? So do not worry, saying, "What shall we eat?" or "What shall we drink?" or "What shall we wear?" For the pagans run after all these things, and your heavenly Father knows that you need them. But seek first his kingdom and his righteousness, and all these things will be given to you as well.'

> Matthew 6:26–33

Jesus said that if we reflected in the right way on created things we would know more about their Creator. The Old Testament said the same thing.

> The heavens declare the glory of God;
> the skies proclaim the work of his hands.

Day after day they pour forth speech;
night after night they display knowledge.
There is no speech or language
where their voice is not heard.
Their voice goes out into all the earth,
their words to the ends of the world.

Psalm 19:1–4

But the glory of God that shines out of the creation
has a dark side to it. A page or two back I mentioned the
heron eating the frogs and fishes in my pond. Since I
began writing this chapter I have led an evening at our
church on 'Spirituality and the Eucharist', and I used
some of the material that I started the chapter with. We
had times for personal reflection and feedback—and
one person picked up the difficulty of the heron eating
the fishes.

'It's all very well to look at the creation,' he said, 'and
for you to say that it shows us something of the Creator.
But what about lions feeding on deer—and all the other
creatures that hunt their prey?'

And it was all very well for me to sit under my
umbrella on a beautiful June day and contemplate the
beauties of creation. What about the rainy days? And
the storms and the floods? And the suffering of the
world?

In the face of those facts the only comfort is that our
God is a suffering God. Not a God who is detached
from his world, but one who is right there in the heart of
it. The prophet Isaiah spoke words that came from
God:

He said, 'Surely they are my people,
sons who will not be false to me';
and so he became their Saviour.

In all their distress he too was distressed,
and the angel of his presence saved them.

But when God the Son hung on a cross, suffering for the sins of the world, God the Father didn't save him. Yet somehow God was in Christ in the suffering, 'reconciling the world to himself in Christ, not counting men's sins against them' (2 Corinthians 5:19).

When we are suffering and desolate, we can know the presence with us of a God who knows suffering—his suffering and our suffering—from the inside. The First World War poet Edward Shillito profoundly (and I believe rightly) rejected the idea that has sometimes been taught by Christians, that the Father turned his back on the Son when he was nailed to the cross in his appalling agony. What did happen then is the deepest mystery of all, and we shall probably never know the depth of it even in the glory of heaven. Edward Shillito wrote a poem about it, called 'The prayer of a Modern Thomas'.

If Thou, O God, the Christ didst leave,
In him, not Thee, do I believe.
To Jesus, dying all alone,
To his dark cross, not Thy bright throne
My hopeless hands will cleave.

But if it was Thy love that died,
Thy voice that in the darkness cried,
The print of nails I long to see
In Thy hands, God who fashioned me.
Show me Thy pierced side.

A God who knows nothing of suffering would be no help to us in ours, and when we were suffering there would be nothing in his nature for us to feed on. But I believe that the creation itself reveals a suffering Creator to us and shows us a self-giving God. If we look in the right way we can see a creation made in the image and likeness of the Creator, just as we human creatures are made in his image and likeness.

When we look at the creation we can see that all things feed on other things. Plants feed on the minerals in the earth. Fish, birds and animals feed on the plants and on other creatures. And human creatures do the same. It is all very well for us to sit down to a Sunday lunch of roast lamb and green peas, and to give thanks to God for his good gifts to us. But what about the lamb? And when we are confronted by a world in which all things feed on other things, what does that tell us about God?

If we have ears to hear, it can tell us the very thing about him that Christianity has always told us. That he is a Creator who gives his own self so that his creatures may take their life from him. God's creation shows us what God is like—and he could no more have made a universe which didn't reveal his nature than Leonardo da Vinci could have painted a bad picture.

The creation we see is one in which all living things take their life from other things. And the God that Christianity tells us about—and whom we see in Jesus—is a God who gives his life for the life of the world. It is a suffering and bleeding world. But then we have a suffering and bleeding God.

Jesus said to them, 'I tell you the truth, unless you can eat the flesh of the Son of Man and drink his blood, you have no life in you. Whoever eats my flesh and drinks my blood has eternal life, and I

Those who eat my flesh and drink my blood abide in me and I in them. John 6:56

I AM THE TRUE VINE

John 15:1

*will raise him up at the last day. For my flesh is
real food and my blood is real drink. Whoever eats
my flesh and drinks my blood remains in me, and I
in him. Just as the living Father sent me and I live
because of the Father, so the one who feeds on me
will live because of me.'*

John 6:53–57

REFLECTIONS FOR 'FEEDING ON THINGS'

- One day when you are eating bread think about how
  it came to you. Imagine the grains of wheat being
  planted in the earth, and growing in the sun and the
  rain. Then being cut down and ground into flour—
  and made into bread for you to eat. Enjoy the taste
  and the texture of it, and think about your body
  digesting it and wonderfully transforming it into
  you.

- Wherever you are, look around you. Perhaps you are
  in a room, or a garden, or a street market. Be aware of
  the colour of things and the shape of things. If there is
  a fly on the window look at it—or at a bird flying.
  Look at the sky, and the clouds. Look at everything
  around you—and be aware how it is entering into you
  as you look, so that you are feeding on the things that
  you see.

- Think about the way the world is, with all things
  living off other things. Reflect on the nature of the
  creation and the Creator God—who gives himself to
  us to feed on.

- Read Edward Shillito's poem again on page 15.
  Think about the suffering of Christ—and reflect on
  the truth that 'God was in Christ reconciling the

world to himself'. Think about someone you know who is suffering, or about a place in the world that you know about where the people are suffering, and turn your thoughts into a prayer.

- Read the verses from Psalm 19 on page 13 and Elizabeth Barrett Browning's poem on page 11. Reflect on the creation as a way through to the Creator and therefore a way of feeding on God.

2

FEEDING ON PEOPLE

I used to have a real problem with holy communion. It didn't mean anything to me and it didn't do anything for me. I much preferred to sing hymns and listen to sermons and readings from the Bible. For me those things were the best way of all to be aware of the glory of God and the wonder of his love and forgiveness. But my feeling about communion niggled away at me, and I thought I had better do something about it.

What I decided to do was to ask a question. Once a month at my church there was a question time after the evening service. The sidesmen would bring round pieces of paper for us to write our questions on, and then they collected them and took them up to the vicar. He had a quick glance through them and selected some suitable ones to answer. One of them turned out to be mine—and since he was very good at answering questions I was full of hope.

He read out from my bit of paper. 'I don't find it helpful to go to communion. Please can you tell me why?' Then he frowned and looked round disapprovingly (and I shrank down into my pew and hoped he hadn't recognized my writing). 'So you don't find it helpful to see your Lord's death portrayed before you!' he said accusingly.

The answer to that question was obviously 'no', because otherwise I wouldn't have asked it. I was irritated. I cannot remember anything else that he said, but as far as I was concerned it was useless. I didn't find communion a help, and I didn't find his answer a help either. And I knew that I wasn't the only person in my church who felt just as I did about the sacrament. But I also knew that Jesus had said, 'Do this in remembrance of me'—so I put the whole thing on a back burner. I waited for a breakthrough and hardly ever went to communion.

Several years later, and very gradually, the break-through happened and I began to understand. It was partly through reading chapter 6 of the Gospel of John. Jesus talks there about eating his flesh and drinking his blood, and as I read his words he seemed to be describing something far greater than the bread and wine of communion. It was more like feeding the whole of my life and being by feeding on his life and being. The heart of chapter 4 of this book is based on that great chapter from John's Gospel. But something else happened to me at the same time, and the two things came together.

I met up with something called Clinical Theology, founded by the late Dr Frank Lake. For the first thirteen years of his working life he had worked in tropical medicine, mainly in parasitology—the study of those living things which live as parasites off the other living things that are their hosts. Nasty things like leeches and intestinal worms, that I prefer not to think about. But I finally found that even those things could lead me into a deeper understanding of relationships—relationships in general and my relationship with God in particular.

Later on Frank Lake worked as a psychiatrist—and moved from internal parasites to inner pain. From what he called 'the study of "internalised bad objects" of the zoological order, to internalised bad object-relationships in the psychological realm': the unhappy memories of bad relationships that people bury deep in their unconscious minds and which cause them severe mental distress.

I went to a two-year course on Clinical Theology and also got hold of a copy of his mammoth book on the subject. It was a life-changing experience for me. There were three things in particular that helped me to change.

I discovered how Christ suffering on the cross could be a living, suffering presence with me in my own suffering, so that I wasn't alone in it any more. When I consider other people's sufferings I realize that I have not suffered very much. Yet I have known various sorts of inner pain—disappointments and rejections that have made me very sad and very unhappy. So sad that sometimes I have gone to sleep crying and woken in the morning still crying. The only comfort when I have been in the depths has been an awareness of the suffering and agony of Christ, sometimes as a presence, or sometimes simply as a truth to believe and hold on to.

I discovered how to pray with total honesty and to dare to be angry in the presence of God and even with God. Lake was writing about people who were suffering from mental stress which was severe enough to take them to a psychiatrist. But all of us suffer from some degree of stress, and when I read the following words they were a real breakthrough for me.

The depressed or afflicted person has stopped praying because he cannot, or feels he cannot, turn either the depravities of rage and lust, or the deprivations of faithlessness, anxiety and emptiness into prayer. Yet because these negative, godless aspects have become for him (though only half-faced as yet) the most important factors defining his identity, he must give full weight to them. He can only do this by seeming to deny the goodness of God's creation and impugning His providence. Unless his self-image of what it is to be a Christian can expand out of all recognition to include, paradoxically, many aspects of personality apparently contrary to faith in God, he will be unable, or feel unable, to pray.

So, prayer as communication with God cannot be re-established unless he can bring his complaints, objections, demands, accusations, resentments, doubts and disbeliefs out of hiding and into conversation with the pastor and with God. But a man cannot say critical things like this to a neurotically conceived god, any more than he can to a neurotically idealised parent. Idealised authorities only want to hear nice things said about themselves. They must be buttered up by saying appreciative things about their ordering of a man's private universe. While this façade is maintained, double-mindedness, hypocrisy, and a loss of energy over the internal conflict and its repression are inevitable. The task of clinical pastoral care is to evoke the truth in the inward parts, however scandalous it may be, so as to bring the total actual content of the personality and its roots into the conversation with God—which is prayer.

Frank Lake, *Clinical Theology*,
Darton, Longman and Todd, 1966

A long quotation with some rather long words. But it transformed my praying. What transformed my whole attitude to holy communion was the way Lake wrote about a new-born baby living a life in union with the mother. The baby doesn't know any life apart from that life-in-union—but the mother nourishes it with the food of love and milk, and its whole life is lived in the light of the love that it sees in her face (or doesn't see—and then the child can be in deep trouble in later life).

But that wasn't all. Lake also wrote of the way Jesus continually went back to the Father to be renewed in himself and in his being.

For Christ, His Spiritual 'Being', as Son of God, arises in a relationship between the Father, Who attends with love, mediated by the Holy Spirit, given to Him without measure, and the Son Who responds to the Father by the same Spirit. Acceptance, for this Holy Son, is always assured. The Son responds by withdrawing alone for prayer, with instant access.

His 'Well-Being' is reached as Christ abides in the Father who gives sustenance to Him at all levels of His Being. The Father, with whom He is united, in prayer and worship and communion, conveys to Him the plenitude of love, glory, joy, grace and truth.

The dynamic outflow of personal 'being' and 'well-being' occurs when the Son of God proceeds forth from the Presence of His Father, full of grace and truth, deeply conscious of His status as the Son of God, to work among men. His motivation is to love as He has been loved.

*His achievement has all the characteristics of the
Holy Spirit's in-dwelling. It is the fulfilment of His
redemptive destiny in history.*

Frank Lake, *Clinical Theology*,
Darton, Longman and Todd, 1966

The whole idea of life lived in relationship with
another, and nourished by another, started to come alive
for me. It was as if I had permission to experiment and to
trust, and to abandon my fear and anxiety about taking
too Catholic a view of the sacrament. The church I went
to would not have approved. But the words of Dr Frank
Lake seemed to set me free.

*The Holy Communion is a Sacrament which
literally carries ontological [which means 'con-
cerning being'] and spiritual strength and sustenance into the life of those who participate in it.
Nowhere is God's Word and act to man, and man's
response by word and act to God, so clearly
demonstrated.*

Frank Lake, *Clinical Theology*,
Darton, Longman and Todd, 1966

I began to realize and experience that feeding on the
bread and the wine was a mystical and spiritual feeding
on the being of Christ. Someone defined a sacrament as
'an outward and visible sign of an inward, spiritual
grace', and that is what it became for me. The person
who is me feeds on the person who is God—and the God
I feed on is like Christ.

It was here that the strange symbolism of Frank
Lake's parasites came alive for me. And I realized that
just as a parasite lives the whole of its life by feeding on

another living being, so I live the whole of my life by feeding on God. When I tried to be independent I was unhappy and out of tune. Now I have accepted my total dependence I delight in it. It doesn't mean that I don't have a life of my own, but that the life I have is a life lived in union with another person, who is my Creator, my Lover, my Saviour and my God.

When we take our life from God and feed on God we are allowing God to enter into us. Not just once at the start of our Christian life—when we are born again of the Spirit (whenever and however that happens, and we may not know the date of our new birth day). God enters into us moment by moment like the breath that we breathe—or like the sap that's the lifeblood of a vine.

> *'I am the true vine, and my Father is the gardener. He cuts off every branch in me that bears no fruit, while every branch that does bear fruit he prunes so that it will be even more fruitful. You are already clean because of the word I have spoken to you. Remain in me, and I will remain in you. No branch can bear fruit by itself; it must remain in the vine. Neither can you bear fruit unless you remain in me. I am the vine; you are the branches. If a man remains in me and I in him, he will bear much fruit; apart from me you can do nothing.'*

> *John 15:1–5*

When we feed on the God who has the nature of Jesus then something extraordinary happens to our human nature—and God gives himself to us and comes to us. Astonishingly, we share in the nature of God:

> *His divine power has given us everything we need for life and godliness through our knowledge of*

*him who called us by his own glory and goodness.
Through these he has given us his very great and
precious promises, so that through them you may
participate in the divine nature ...*

2 Peter 1:3–4

At the start of the last century Henry Scougal wrote a
book called *The Life of God in the Soul of Man*. And that
is what Christianity is. The Apostle Paul wrote about
the 'glorious riches of this mystery, which is Christ in
you, the hope of glory'. And he says, 'So then, just as
you received Christ Jesus as Lord, continue to live in
him, rooted and built up in him, strengthened in the
faith as you were taught, and overflowing with thankfulness' (Colossians 1:27; 2:6–7).

In a way we all 'feed' on people, and other people
feed on us. We look at each other and we speak to each
other—sharing our hopes, our dreams and our fears as
well as the everyday, ordinary, things that have been
happening in our lives.

In the musical *The King and I*, the king's children
and Anna, their new nurse, sing a song together:
'Getting to know you. Getting to know all about you.'
And doing that is a sort of feeding. The things that the
other person knows about enter into us and become part
of us—and then we tell them about the things that we
know. We don't ever know all about another person.
But as we listen we get to know more—and as we open
up to them about ourselves they get to know more about
us.

There is more to listening than just hearing another
person's words. It has to do with noticing their body
language, and how they turn towards us, or away from
us. It is also about looking at the expression on their
face—and if a person looks down on us and despises us it

is is like drinking a sort of poison. When someone is pleased to see us we know it—and the feeling they have for us enters into us and makes us feel good, and we know that we matter to them.

The Old Testament talks about the face of God. The writers know that they can't see it with their physical eyes, yet they can with the eyes of faith. Right back at the beginning, God tells Moses how Aaron the priest is to give a blessing to the people:

> The Lord said to Moses, 'Tell Aaron and his sons, "This is how you are to bless the Israelites. Say to them:
>
> The Lord bless you
> and keep you;
> the Lord make his face shine upon you
> and be gracious to you;
> the Lord turn his face towards you
> and give you peace."'

Numbers 6:22–26

Imagine the whole of our life lived in the shining light of the loving face of God, turned towards us and giving us his peace. Not a God whom we can see with the eyes in our face, but whom we can see with the eyes of our heart. And when we look at another person in the right way, or if they look at us, that can be an experience of seeing the face of God. In that marvellous musical *Les Misérables* one of the songs says that 'to love another person is to see the face of God', and I wonder if the writer got the idea from the story of Jacob in the Old Testament.

Jacob saw the face of God twice. His brother Esau was on his way to meet him with four hundred men, and

Jacob was frightened. He faced an unknown situation that he couldn't control—although he had done his best to pacify Esau with presents. Waiting and alone, he must have asked himself what he had been struggling for all his life. Then, in the darkness, a mysterious man comes and wrestles with him until just before daybreak. When the man sees that he isn't winning, he strikes Jacob on the hip and throws it out of joint.

> Then the man said, 'Let me go, for it is daybreak.'
> But Jacob replied, 'I will not let you go unless you bless me.'
> The man asked him, 'What is your name?'
> 'Jacob,' he answered.
> Then the man said, 'Your name will no longer be Jacob, but Israel, because you have struggled with God and with men and have overcome.'
> Jacob said, 'Please tell me your name.'
> But he replied, 'Why do you ask my name?' Then he blessed him there.
> So Jacob called the place Peniel, saying, 'It is because I saw God face to face, and yet my life was spared.'

Genesis 32:26–30

Jacob had seen the face of God in that transforming meeting at the end of that long night. Then he sees it again—in the face of his brother. Esau had once been his enemy and planned to kill him, because Jacob had twisted him out of his inheritance. In the light of this new day, Jacob urges Esau to keep the present he has brought for him, even though Esau says he doesn't need it. Jacob is a changed man, and after looking into the face of God he looks into his brother's face with new eyes: 'If I have found favour in your eyes, accept this gift from me. For to see your face is like seeing the face of God' (Genesis 33:10).

When we see someone we love after a long time it is as if we feast our eyes on each other's faces. We look at the features of the person we love, and at the love and kindness in their eyes. And something within us is deeply satisfied—with something far better than food.

When lovers are with each other they delight in each other in a mutual happiness—and the love song that is right at the heart of the Bible has just the right words for it:

> Let him kiss me with the kisses of his mouth—
> for your love is more delightful than wine.
> How delightful is your love, my sister my
> bride!
> How much more pleasing is your love than wine,
> and the fragrance of your perfume than any spice!
> Your lips drop sweetness as the honeycomb, my
> bride;
> milk and honey are under your tongue . . .
> I have come into my garden, my sister, my
> bride;
> I have gathered my myrrh with my spice.
> I have eaten my honeycomb and my honey;
> I have drunk my wine and my milk.
> Eat, O friends, and drink;
> drink your fill, O lovers.

> Song of Songs 1:2; 4:10–11; 5:1

Their love-making is sweeter than honey and better than wine and, in the love songs of the Song of Solomon, Jews and Christians have always seen an allegory of the love relationship between God and his beloved people.

What can separate us from the love of CHRIST? Rom. 8:35

For Christians, Christ is the bridegroom and the Church is his bride—and heaven is going to be a marriage supper. In the vision which God gives to John on the island of Patmos, he shows him what is going to happen in the future:

> Then I heard what sounded like a great multitude, like the roar of rushing waters and like loud peals of thunder, shouting:
> 'Hallelujah!
> For our Lord God Almighty reigns.
> Let us rejoice and be glad
> and give him glory!
> For the wedding of the Lamb has come,
> and his bride has made herself ready.
> Fine linen, bright and clean,
> was given her to wear.'
> (Fine linen stands for the righteous acts of the saints).
> Then the angel said to me, 'Write: "Blessed are those who are invited to the wedding supper of the Lamb!"' And he added, 'These are the true words of God.'

Revelation 19:6–9

We can feed on God through the words of God, and that is what we shall reflect on in the next chapter.

REFLECTIONS FOR 'FEEDING ON PEOPLE'

- Imagine a baby in its mother's arms. See the child feeding—and see the love in the mother's eyes as she looks at her child. Think of the glory of God in the face of Jesus Christ—and imagine how he looks at you.

- Think about a parasite living on its host—taking all its life and nourishment from the host that it is feeding on. Be honest about your feelings as you reflect on the parasite—and then reflect on your own life, totally dependent on God, in whom 'we live and move and have our being' (Acts 17:28).

- Read the quotation from Dr Frank Lake on page 24. Then pray as openly as you can about everything that is in your heart. Over the months and years ahead, go on praying in this way—so that your communication with God gets better and better. As you speak to him like this you will discover that you hear him speaking to you more clearly, because now you don't have to hide anything any more, and nothing is unmentionable.

3

FEEDING ON WORDS

The first time that I went to Coventry Cathedral I was awestruck. As I entered through the great glass doors the enormous archangels engraved on them made me aware of my smallness and of God's immensity. The feeling of size and space inside the building deepened that awareness, and I knew the delighted humility of being a creature of the God who is my Creator and lover.

Inside the cathedral I saw the light streaming through the dark stained-glass windows by Piper, and the crown of spiked thorns in the chapel of Christ the Servant. I gazed up at Christ in majesty in the great Sutherland tapestry over the holy table, and it was as if the glory of God streamed out of the picture. I found myself worshipping with the whole company of heaven:

> 'Worthy is the Lamb, who was slain,
> to receive power and wealth and wisdom and strength
> and honour and glory and praise!'
> Then I heard every creature in heaven and on
> earth and under the earth and on the sea, and all
> that is in them, singing:

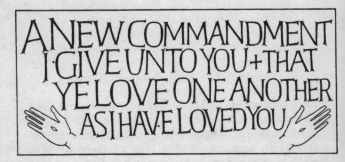

'To him who sits on the throne and to the Lamb
be praise and honour and glory and power,
for ever and ever!'

Revelation 5:12–13

That was the height of my experience of wonder and
delight. But before it there had been another, which had
gone right to the depth of me. Set into the interior walls
of the cathedral there are eight stone tablets. Known as
The Tablets of the Word, they each have a verse from
the Bible engraved into the stone, and all except one has
a simple picture to illustrate the words.

As I stood in front of one tablet it was as if the words
and the picture carved on the stone were being cut deep
into my heart. 'A new commandment I give unto you.
That ye love one another as I have loved you.' Under
the words the outlines of two hands were carved out,
with a wound gouged out deep in both palms. I was
delighted and appalled at the same time. Delighted with
an awareness of the astonishing love with which I was
loved by God. Appalled by the almost impossible
loving that Christ was demanding from me.

Words are powerful, and so are pictures. They enter
into us and become part of us—like food and like
feeding. For the ancient Jews, a word had its own
existence and it went off and did things. In the Old
Testament, Jacob tricks his brother out of his blessing
by pretending to his blind father, Isaac, that he is Esau.
Encouraged and helped by his mother he wears his
brother's clothes and puts skins on his hands (because
Esau had hairy hands and he didn't). It was a terrible
deception. But once Isaac had given Jacob his blessing
he couldn't take it back. He had spoken the words, and
they had started to act.

But, for the Jews, it wasn't only human beings who spoke. God spoke a word that brought the whole universe into existence. A Jew once wrote a letter to other Jews (the Epistle to the Hebrews) and referred to the word of God and what it did: 'By faith we understand that the world was created by the word of God, so that what is seen was made out of things which do not appear' (Hebrews 11:3, RSV).

At the beginning of the Bible there is an account of the beginning of the world—and every time God speaks his word something else is brought into being:

> In the beginning God created the heavens and the earth. Now the earth was formless and empty, darkness was over the surface of the deep, and the Spirit of God was hovering over the waters. And God said, 'Let there be light,' and there was light.
>
> Genesis 1:1–3

God goes on speaking, and the creation goes on happening. There is a beautiful account of it in one of C.S. Lewis's children's stories, when Aslan creates the country of Narnia.

> The Lion was pacing to and fro about that empty land and singing his new song. It was softer and more lilting than the song by which he had called up the stars and the sun; a gentle, rippling music. And as he walked and sang the valley grew green with grass. It spread out from the Lion like a pool. It ran up the sides of the little hills like a wave . . . Soon there were other things besides grass . . . Showers of birds came out of the trees. Butterflies fluttered. Bees got to work on the flowers as if they hadn't a second to lose . . .

Then there came a swift flash like fire (but it burnt nobody) either from the sky or from the Lion itself, and every drop of blood tingled in the children's bodies, and the deepest, wildest voice they had ever heard was saying:

'Narnia, Narnia, Narnia, awake. Love. Think. Speak. Be walking trees. Be talking beasts. Be divine waters.'

C.S. Lewis, *The Magician's Nephew*,
HarperCollins © 1955

The word of God is full of power, and it was that word which people recognized when Jesus spoke to them here on earth. When he went into the synagogue in Capernaum, Mark says that 'the people were amazed at his teaching, because he taught them as one who had authority, not as the teachers of the law' (Mark 1:22). And it wasn't only human beings who recognized the authority in his words.

Just then a man in their synagogue who was possessed by an evil spirit cried out, 'What do you want with us, Jesus of Nazareth? Have you come to destroy us? I know who you are—the Holy One of God!'

'Be quiet!' said Jesus sternly. 'Come out of him!' The evil spirit shook the man violently and came out of him with a shriek.

Mark 1:23–26

Then Mark says that the people were all so amazed that they asked each other, 'What is this? A new teaching—and with authority! He even gives orders to evil spirits and they obey him' (Mark 1:27).

39

Three of the most powerful words in the world are 'I love you.' When we're in love we want hear them said to us and we want to say them to the person we love. But we don't even need to be in love. A child wants to hear them from its parents—and a mother or a father wants to say them to their child. We can say 'I love you' to a friend—and our friend can say it to us—although we're more likely to put it in another way and say, 'I really like being with you,' or, 'I'm really glad I know you.' I said that to someone yesterday, and I heard a smile in his voice over the telephone. 'That makes me feel all nice and warm inside,' he said. And I felt the same, because I had said it.

There are different sorts of loving for different sorts of relationships. The same in some ways and different in other ways. If we love someone we want to be with them for some or for most of the time—depending on the sort of loving and on how much we love. There are different sorts of loving: sexual love and friendship love and family love. And in each relationship we want to say 'I love you' to the other and hear the other say 'I love you' to us. We can show another person that we love them by the things that we do—but to say the words as well doubles up on the action.

Three intensely powerful and life-giving words— and it isn't only human beings who say them. God says them—to the whole world in general and to every individual in particular: 'I have loved you with an everlasting love.'

But now, this is what the Lord says—
he who created you, O Jacob,
he who formed you, O Israel:
'Fear not, for I have redeemed you;
I have summoned you by name; you are mine.
When you pass through the waters,

40

I will be with you;
and when you pass through the rivers,
they will not sweep over you.
When you walk through the fire,
you will not be burned;
the flames will not set you ablaze.
For I am the Lord, your God,
the Holy One of Israel, your Saviour;
I give Egypt for your ransom,
Cush and Seba in your stead.
Since you are precious and honoured in my sight,
and because I love you . . .'

Isaiah 43:1–4

But it wasn't Egypt that the Saviour God gave for our ransom. It was himself.

'For God so loved the world that he gave his one
and only Son, that whoever believes in him shall
not perish but have eternal life. For God did not
send his Son into the world to condemn the world,
but to save the world through him.'

John 3:16–17

Back in the twelfth century, St Bernard of Clairvaux said that whenever he looked at a crucifix the five wounds of Christ appeared to him as five lips, speaking the words 'I love you.'

We can feed on the words—and as the words enter into us so does the wonder of the truth. We can listen to the words of God and get to know them, and as we do we shall be nourished and fed.

Two Sundays ago I was at a confirmation service in Chichester Cathedral, where one of my godsons was being confirmed. The bishop who took the service said that many Church members are undernourished—and he was talking about the nourishment that we get from the sacrament of holy communion and from feeding on the word of God. Like the words that God gave to the prophet Ezekiel to eat:

'Son of man, listen to what I say to you. Do not rebel like that rebellious house; open your mouth and eat what I give you.' Then I looked, and I saw a hand stretched out to me. In it was a scroll, which he unrolled before me. On both sides of it were written words of lament and mourning and woe. And he said to me, 'Son of man, eat . . . this scroll; then go and speak to the house of Israel.' So I opened my mouth, and he gave me the scroll to eat. Then he said to me, 'Son of man, eat this scroll I am giving you and fill your stomach with it.' So I ate it, and it tasted as sweet as honey in my mouth.

Ezekiel 2:8—3:3

Ezekiel had to listen and to eat, and the word of God entered into him and became part of him, so that he spoke the words of God to his generation—and to ours as well. We can still feed ourselves on those ancient words, and they are as life-giving today as they ever were. And the Bible continually uses the imagery of eating and drinking to talk about our feeding on God and on the words of God.

Come, all you who are thirsty,
come to the waters;
and you who have no money,
come, buy and eat!
Come, buy wine and milk

without money and without cost.
Why spend money on what is not bread,
and your labour on what does not satisfy?
Listen, listen to me, and eat what is good,
and your soul will delight in the richest of fare.
Give ear and come to me;
hear me, that your soul may live.

Isaiah 55:1–3

In Peter's first letter, the word of God is both a seed that grows into a new life within us and also the food to nourish that new life. A new Christian is like a newborn baby—and the word of God is like milk.

. . . you have been born again, not of perishable seed, but of imperishable, through the living and enduring word of God. For,
   'All men are like grass,
and all their glory is like the flowers of the field;
the grass withers and the flowers fall,
but the word of the Lord stands for ever.'
   And this is the word that was preached to you.
   Therefore, rid yourselves of all malice and all deceit, hypocrisy, envy, and slander of every kind. Like newborn babies, crave pure spiritual milk, so that by it you may grow up in your salvation, now that you have tasted that the Lord is good.

1 Peter 1:23—2:3

Earlier this year I bought two packets of nicotiana seeds. There was a picture of the full-grown tobacco plant on the front of the packets and details about it on the back: four to five feet high and very sweet smelling. It was the smell that I wanted them for—to plant underneath my front window so that on summer evenings the scent from the big white flowers will fill my room. But because I am not very good at growing seeds two friends took the two packets and grew them for me.

Two thousand tiny, black seeds in each packet—and now, after the dying in potting compost, and the growing up towards the light, there are masses of tobacco plants growing in my garden. Not flowering yet, so not yet scenting my room with their marvellous fragrance. But on their way—like us as Christians. Starting very small, but then growing up to the light—and then, one day, being able to say what Paul said and, like him, giving all the glory and thanks to God as we say it:

> But thanks be to God, who always leads us in triumphal procession in Christ and through us spreads everywhere the fragrance of the knowledge of him. For we are to God the aroma of Christ among those who are being saved and those who are perishing. To the one we are the smell of death; to the other, the fragrance of life.

> 2 Corinthians 2:14–16

A seed is like a word, with an astonishing possibility contained within it. We have to let it enter us and take root in us, and then the new life starts to grow. Tiny in its beginning, like a newly-conceived child, and like a new-born baby. The apostle Paul wrote about the new life of the new creation——brought into being through the word of God just as the world was brought into being.

> For we do not preach ourselves, but Jesus Christ as Lord, and ourselves as your servants for Jesus'

sake. For God, who said, 'Let light shine out of darkness,' made his light shine in our hearts to give us the light of the knowledge of the glory of God in the face of Christ.

2 Corinthians 4:5–6

In another letter to those Christians in Corinth, Paul was saying very much what that bishop in Chichester Cathedral was saying. The bishop said a lot of people in our church were undernourished because they weren't taking enough food. Paul said that they were unspiritual and immature for the same reason.

Brothers, I could not address you as spiritual but as worldly—mere infants in Christ. I gave you milk, not solid food, for you were not yet ready for it. Indeed, you are still not ready. You are still worldly. For since there is jealousy and quarrelling among you, are you not worldly?

1 Corinthians 3:1–3

It says much the same thing, but in even tougher words, in the letter to Jewish Christians. The toughness isn't surprising. It is the concern of a loving parent who wants a child to grow up to be a mature human being instead of getting stuck as an undeveloped infant.

We have much to say about this [the priesthood of Christ], but it is hard to explain because you are slow to learn. In fact, though by this time you ought to be teachers, you need someone to teach you the elementary truths of God's word all over again. You need milk, not solid food! Anyone who

*lives on milk, being still an infant, is not
acquainted with the teaching about righteous-
ness. But solid food is for the mature, who by
constant use have trained themselves to
distinguish good from evil.*

Hebrews 5:11–14

The solid food that we have to feed on is God
himself—not just the words about God that are there
in the Bible and in the Creeds. And yet without the
words we shall not be able to know God, because we
shall not know what he is like. Jesus used words to tell
us—in the parables that are stories about the nature of
God. Some of the religious establishment of the day
didn't like either what Jesus did or the stories that he
told.

*Now the tax collectors and 'sinners' were all
gathering round to hear him. But the Pharisees
and the teachers of the law muttered, 'This man
welcomes sinners, and eats with them.'
   Then Jesus told them this parable: 'Suppose
one of you has a hundred sheep and loses one of
them. Does he not leave the ninety-nine in the
open country and go after the lost sheep until he
finds it? And when he finds it, he joyfully puts it
on his shoulders and goes home. Then he calls his
friends and neighbours together and says, "Re-
joice with me; I have found my lost sheep." I tell
you that in the same way there will be more
rejoicing in heaven over one sinner who repents
than over ninety-nine righteous persons who do
not need to repent.'*

Luke 15:1–7

Words to tell a story about God—and in the telling of it to give us some very good news. I love the old hymn about the the Lord who went to look for his lost sheep.

Lord, Thou hast in Thy fold Thy ninety and nine,
Are they not enough for Thee?
But the Shepherd made answer,
'This of Mine has wandered away from Me.
And although the way be rough and steep
I go to the desert, to find My sheep.'

But none of the ransomed ever knew
How deep were the waters crossed,
Or how dark the night that the Lord went through
To rescue His sheep that was lost.

The whole of that wonderful chapter of Luke's Gospel is about lost things that finally get found by God. A woman searches for a coin that is lost, and when she finds it she calls her friends and neighbours in to be glad that she has found it. And Jesus says, 'In the same way, I tell you, there is rejoicing in the presence of the angels of God over one sinner who repents' (Luke 15:10).

The last story in the chapter is the best of all. About a son who leaves home for a far country, and a father who waits and longs for him to come back again. One day, out in the field with the pigs, the son comes to his senses and decides to go home. His motivation isn't very exalted. The fact of the matter is that he is very hungry—and he remembers the food that he could eat back in his father's house. So he sets out to go home— and on the way he works out what he is going to say: 'Father, I have sinned against heaven and against you. I am no longer worthy to be called your son; make me like one of your hired men.'

But he doesn't manage to get it all out, because when he is still a long way off his father sees him and comes rushing out to meet him. He throws his arms round him and kisses him—and, held in his father's arms, the son says, 'Father, I have sinned against heaven and against you. I am no longer worthy to be called your son.' He doesn't get out his suggestion about being a slave, because the father is so delighted that he throws a party for him. The father says to the servants:

> 'Bring the fattened calf and kill it. Let's have a feast and celebrate. For this son of mine was dead and is alive again; he was lost and is found.'

Luke 15:23–24

If God is really like that—and that's the whole point of what Jesus was saying—then Christianity is the most wonderfully good news. The words of the story tell us what God is like—and we can feed on them to our heart's content. God is like that, and God is like Jesus. The New Testament says that Jesus is the Word of God and the Word that God has spoken to us:

> In the past God spoke to our forefathers through the prophets at many times and in various ways, but in these last days he has spoken to us by his Son, whom he appointed heir of all things, and through whom he made the universe. The Son is the radiance of God's glory and the exact representation of his being, sustaining all things by his powerful word.

Hebrews 1:1–3

I have loved you with an everlasting love — Jer. 31.3

God is like Jesus, and we have a Christ-like God. In his superb book *Making Sense out of Suffering*, Peter Kreeft writes about the wonder of the Christian story and how God entered our world.

It is, of course, the most familar, the most often-told story in the world. Yet it is also the strangest, and it has never lost its strangeness, its awe, and will not even in eternity, where angels tremble to gaze at things we yawn at. And however strange, it is the only key that fits the lock of our tortured lives and needs. We needed a surgeon, and he came and reached into our wounds with bloody hands. He didn't give us a placebo or a pill or good advice. He gave us himself.

He came. He entered space and time and suffering. He came, like a lover. Love seeks above all intimacy, presence, togetherness. Not happiness. 'Better unhappy with her than happy without her'—that is the word of a lover. He came. That is the salient fact, the towering truth, that alone keeps us from putting a bullet through our heads. He came. Job is satisfied even though the God who came gave him absolutely no answers at all to his thousand tortured questions. He did the most important thing and he gave the most important gift: himself. It is a lover's gift. Out of our tears, our waiting, our darkness, our agonized aloneness, out of our weeping and wondering, out of our cry, 'My God, my God, why hast Thou forsaken me?' he came, all the way, right into that cry.

Peter Kreeft, *Making Sense out of Suffering*

St John tells us who came and how he came.

In the beginning was the Word, and the Word was with God, and the Word was God . . . The Word became flesh and made his dwelling among us.

John 1:1, 14

REFLECTIONS FOR 'FEEDING ON WORDS'

- Look at the words of Jesus in the picture of the panel from Coventry Cathedral—and look at the hands underneath the words. Let the words and the picture sink into you—and then reflect on what they are saying to you.

- Read out the hymn on page 48—'Lord, Thou hast in Thy fold Thy ninety and nine . . .' and let the pictures that the words evoke come into your mind. Reflect on them—and consider what they are saying to you about the Lord who is our shepherd.

- Read the story of the prodigal son on page 48 and let the words paint a picture for you. Imagine the son in the field . . . imagine the father waiting at home. Reflect on the words that he said: 'This son of mine was dead and is alive again.'

- Read the quotation from Peter Kreeft's *Making Sense out of Suffering* on page 51 and then spend some time reflecting on the pictures that the words bring into your mind. Become aware of how you are being nourished by the words of the story.

4

FEEDING ON GOD

It is Sunday morning and I am sitting up in my bed writing. I try not to work on Sundays, but sometimes I do so when I have to meet a deadline. In two hours time I shall be in church eating the bread and drinking the wine of communion—the sacrament that is the outward and visible and sign of an inward and spiritual grace. I shall be doing what the words of the service tell me to do: 'Eat and drink in remembrance that he died for you, and feed on him in your heart by faith with thanksgiving.'

FEEDING ON GOD THROUGH THINGS

But I am also feeding on God now—and what I am trying to do is to work out how I am doing it. I am looking out of my bedroom window at the sky and the hills and the trees—and delighting in the greyness of the sky and the shape of the hills and the rich yellows and oranges of late October. A deep thankfulness to the creator God who made all these things is welling up inside me as I look—and in 'Feeding on things' I shared with you something of the way that created things lead me into worship.

FEEDING ON GOD THROUGH PEOPLE

Now I am remembering the people I talked to last night at a friend's birthday party. Most of them have been friends of mine for nearly twenty years—and before I began to write (or, more accurately, re-write) this chapter I was praying and saying, 'Thank you, Lord, for all of them'—and I was remembering their faces and their personalities as I prayed. Then I was thanking God for this place where I live. For my little house that looks up to the hills—and for all the people whom I know in my town. I am feeding on God through people.

FEEDING ON GOD THROUGH WORDS

I was also praying some words from the Bible that have been in my heart all week. They come from the 'Sentences' at the start of Morning Prayer (which I say and pray most mornings) and I spotted this one right at the end. It is for a dedication—the words that Jacob said when he lay down in the desert and put his head on a stone to sleep. Then he had a dream, and saw a stairway which reached from heaven to earth, with angels going up and down on it, and the Lord standing there beside him and speaking to him.

The translation could mean that the Lord was at the top of the staircase and speaking to Jacob at the bottom—but I believe that the reality was that God was very close to him when he spoke. The Lord made the same promise to him that he had made to his grandfather Abraham—and the heart of the promise was that God would be with him wherever he went, and that all the people on earth would be blessed through him.

Then Jacob woke up from his dream with an awareness of the presence of the living God—and he said

'Surely the Lord is in this place . . . This is none other than the house of God; this is the gate of heaven' (Genesis 28:16–17). I have been thinking a lot about those words every morning since Monday, and realizing that they are true for all places and for all people. I am feeding on God through things, through people and through words.

So all those things are happening inside my head and inside me—but they aren't the whole of what is happening. Springing up from deep inside me—like a well of delight and happiness—there is an awareness of the presence of God with me and within me. I am living a life in union and communion with Christ in me—and my whole life and being is drawing itself in great joy from the God who is here within me—as well as out there holding all the stars in the galaxies of the Milky Way in existence. And I am thinking again of that extraordinary image that Frank Lake used of the parasite which takes its whole life from its host. But a parasite is an unpleasant image for most of us—and to live on God is the height and the totality of all pleasure and happiness.

THE LIFE OF GOD

'All my springs are in you,' says Psalm 87:7 (RSV), and Psalm 46:4 says that 'There is a river whose streams make glad the city of God'. The springs and the river are the life of God himself—the source of our life and of all our joy. The life of God in us—feeding our life with his own and with himself. The God who is the river of life and the bread of life—for us to swim in and to feed on.

No single image is rich enough to describe what the life of God is like—and even the best images are not the reality of God himself. Thomas Traherne put two images together to try to put the glory into words:

I within did flow
With seas of life, like wine.

'Wonder', iii

A sea that can intoxicate us and a presence that we can exult in—in union and communion. But in our human life here on this earth our eyes are often flowing with tears. God knows all about our tears, though, and it says that one day he will wipe them all away from our eyes, and that then there will be no more death or mourning or crying or pain. For now he is here with us in our weeping and our sorrow. The crucified God and the suffering God—and we know him in the suffering of Christ. Suffering with us in all our distress—and sustaining us in all our pain. Not taking the pain away—but with us in the anguish of it.

There was a love song in the British charts a few years ago. The first line of it was 'Always there! Love will be always there!' And it will. Our human loves will be there as best they can, though always partially. But the love of God will be always there for us, totally present, in our joy and in our pain—loving us, feeding us, forgiving us, and giving us his life.

That is what Jesus said he would do for us. He said it all through his ministry—and to say it was also to say that he was more than a man.

FEEDING ON JESUS

Right at the heart of the Christian Gospel there is an outrageous, barely believable, and totally satisfying announcement about human beings feeding on God. This announcement wasn't made by God speaking through the prophets. It was made by God in person standing on the shore of the Sea of Galilee—the Word who became flesh speaking words that told us for all time about the wonder of the self-giving, life-giving love of God.

Jesus told the people listening to him that they could feed on him, and that if they did they would live for ever. If they didn't then they weren't really alive at all— and what he said to them is just as true for us.

> Jesus said to them, 'I tell you the truth, unless you can eat the flesh of the Son of Man and drink his blood, you have no life in you. Whoever eats my flesh and drinks my blood has eternal life, and I will raise him up at the last day. For my flesh is real food and my blood is real drink. Whoever eats my flesh and drinks my blood remains in me, and I in him. Just as the living Father sent me and I live because of the Father, so the one who feeds on me will live because of me. This is the bread that came down from heaven. Your forefathers ate manna and died, but he who feeds on this bread will live for ever.'

> John 6:53–58

There is food for the body and food for the soul—and the day before Jesus said these mysterious things to the crowds by the Sea of Galilee he had given them food for their bodies. In the feeding of the five thousand a boy had given him five small loaves and two small fishes. Hopelessly inadequate supplies for all the people who were there. Humanly speaking, that is. But this was more than a human story. This was the Creator God in human form, and God the Son took the bread and the fishes into his hands and gave thanks to God the Father. Then he gave the bread and fishes to the people. They were hungry, so he fed them—with enough food to satisfy their hunger totally and then some left over.

But the next morning the people were hungry again, so they set out to look for Jesus. They found him on the other side of the lake—and they were probably thinking hungrily about there being more bread and fishes for breakfast. There wasn't. Instead, Jesus gave them a profound piece of metaphysical teaching about feeding on God, and they found it very hard.

> When they found him on the other side of the lake, they asked him, 'Rabbi, when did you get here?'
> Jesus answered, 'I tell you the truth, you are looking for me, not because you saw miraculous signs but because you ate the loaves and had your fill. Do not work for food that spoils, but for food that endures to eternal life, which the Son of Man will give you. On him God the Father has placed his seal of approval.'

> John 6:25–27

FOOD THAT LASTS FOR EVER

I have just had to throw away four little cartons of delicious gooseberry fool that I bought last week from Marks & Spencer's. At least, they would have been delicious, just like the last lot—creamy, with a beautiful delicate flavour. But this lot had passed its sell-by date. It was spoilt. So now it's in the bin.

But what is Jesus talking about when he says, 'Do not work for food that spoils, but for food that endures to eternal life'—food that he says he will give to us?

His puzzled listeners understand the word 'work' so they home in on that. 'What must we do to do the works God requires?' The answer to that one is to believe in Jesus. So then they want a sign. Why should they believe? What will Jesus do to prove who he is?

The Jews always remembered their Exodus from Egypt, when God led them out of slavery into the freedom of the Promised Land. On their journey they had gone through a dry desert of a place, and wandered round in this wilderness for forty years (because they hadn't had the faith or the courage to do what God told them to do at the start). In the wilderness they had been fed on manna—little white flakes that they found on the ground every morning and made into bread.

Moses was the man who had led them into the wilderness, so they believed it was through him that they had food to eat when they were hungry. They quoted their scriptures. 'As it is written: "He gave them bread from heaven to eat." ' So what will Jesus give them?

He starts to lead them deep into the truth about God and about himself. Because of what happened the day before they are thinking about eating bread. And they have remembered in their own sacred history about a special bread that came down from heaven. They knew that that bread had gone off and gone maggotty by the next morning. But Jesus says that there is another sort of bread—living bread—and if anyone eats it they will live for ever. Astonishingly, and almost unbelievably, Jesus tells them that he himself is this bread.

'I tell you the truth, it is not Moses who has given you the bread from heaven, but it is my Father who gives you the true bread from heaven. For the bread of God is he who comes down from heaven and gives life to the world.'

John 6:32–33

Dimly, they are starting to understand—or some of them are—and they want what he is offering them.

60

'Sir,' they said, 'from now on give us this bread.'
Then Jesus declared, 'I am the bread of life. He
who comes to me will never go hungry, and he
who believes in me will never be thirsty.'

John 6:34–35

He was making outrageous claims for himself—and
they started saying things to each other about him. Who
does he think he is? 'Is this not Jesus, the son of Joseph,
whose father and mother we know? How can he now
say, "I came down from heaven?"'

Jesus tells them to stop grumbling—and then says
even more astonishing things about the way that people
will be drawn to him and what he will do for them when
they come to him.

THE BREAD OF LIFE

'No one can come to me unless the Father who
sent me draws him, and I will raise him up at the
last day. It is written in the Prophets: "They will
all be taught by God." Everyone who listens to the
Father and learns from him comes to me. No-one
has seen the Father except the one who is from
God; only he has seen the Father. I tell you the
truth, he who believes has everlasting life. I am
the bread of life. Your forefathers ate the manna in
the desert, yet they died. But here is the bread that
comes down from heaven, which a man may eat
and not die. I am the living bread that came down
from heaven. If anyone eats of this bread, he will
live for ever. This bread is my flesh, which I will
give for the life of the world.'

John 6:44–51

They asked the inevitable question—and it is the question to which we all yearn to know the answer. Not just in theory but in practice—because once we really know it then we can eat and drink from the source of all being and all delight to our heart's content.

> Then the Jews began to argue sharply among themselves, 'How can this man give us his flesh to eat?'

John 6:52

BLOOD AND DEATH

It wasn't easy for them to understand. We can look back to the glory and the agony of Good Friday and know something of what Jesus meant. But for them Good Friday lay in the future—the day when the grain of wheat would fall into the ground and die, so that there would be many grains. When Jesus talked to them about eating his flesh and drinking his blood they would have been in a turmoil, because they were totally forbidden to consume animal blood, let alone human blood. The key to a partial understanding of what he was saying was there in their own scriptures—but they would only be able to unlock the mystery after his death.

> 'Any Israelite or any alien living among them who eats any blood—I will set my face against that person who eats blood and will cut him off from his people. For the life of a creature is in the blood, and I have given it to you to make atonement for yourselves on the altar; it is the blood that makes atonement for one's life . . . Any Israelite or any alien living among you who hunts any animal or

bird that may be eaten must drain out the blood and cover it with earth, because the life of every creature is its blood.

Leviticus 17:10–14

The connection between blood and death was awesome. The life blood of Jesus would be shed in an atoning sacrifice for sin when he died on the cross—and then they would be able to drink his blood, and know within themselves 'the benefits of his death and passion'.

The dripping blood our only drink,
The bloody flesh our only food;
In spite of which we like to think
That we are sound, substantial flesh and blood—
Again, in spite of that, we call this Friday good.

T.S. Eliot, 'East Coker',
Four Quartets, Faber and Faber

John the Baptist saw to the heart of it. When he saw Jesus coming towards him he said 'Look, the Lamb of God, who takes away the sin of the world!' (John 1:29)—and what he had in mind was the Passover lamb that was killed and eaten every year at the feast. It was a looking back to the Jews' sacred history.

The night before they left the slavery of Egypt to go to the freedom of the Promised Land they were warned that the angel of death would pass through the whole land and kill all the first-born sons—Egyptian sons and Jewish sons. But the Jewish families were to kill a lamb, and put the blood on the door of their houses. Then, when the angel of death saw the blood, he would pass over that place.

The whole story, Jewish and Christian, is about an innocent victim being a substitute for someone else, who isn't innocent. The victim's death for someone else's life, because the someone else is loved by God and is dying.

When Jesus told people they had to eat his flesh and drink his blood they were shocked and bewildered. But when we are emotionally shaken and disturbed we can sometimes see the truth of things that we never saw before, and we are open to receive new information. It doesn't always work like that. Sometimes we get so upset that we close our minds and run away and hide—so that we don't have to change.

Some of the people who heard what Jesus said were brave enough to change—but only after his death and resurrection and the pouring out of the Spirit at Pentecost. All those things had to happen first, before they could really understand and experience what he was telling them.

Then he would enter into them in a new and mysterious way—so much a part of them that there were only two ways to talk about it and describe it. One was through food and drink, and the other was through spirit.

Earlier in the Gospel of John, Jesus talked to the woman at the well in Samaria about the Spirit. She had had five husbands and was currently set up with a live-in lover. A lifestyle rather like that of millions of men and women in the Western world. Searching for happiness in the wrong places. Regularly breaking the seventh commandment. Laughing at the television comedies with their regular storylines of extra-marital sex and deception.

Broken commandments result in broken hearts. But God is the one who binds up the brokenhearted—however the breaking happened. This woman was a sinner. But Jesus didn't start with her sin. He started with her—and he offered her water to quench the real thirst and longing that was in her soul. He asked her to give him a drink from Jacob's well, and presumably she did—although she was surprised that he talked to her.

Jews never talked to Samaritans, and a good law-abiding Jew would never have spoken to a woman in the street at all, let alone a woman like this one. But Jesus did. He talked to her about himself and about God—and gave her one of the most wonderful lessons in theology that there has ever been. He started just where she was—and just where he was. Both of them thirsty—but now his thirst was being quenched with the water she had given to him. Then—perhaps with her bucket of cold, refreshing water held on his knee—Jesus told her about another sort of water.

'Everyone who drinks this water will be thirsty again, but whoever drinks the water I give him

will never thirst. Indeed, the water I give him will become in him a spring of water welling up to eternal life.'

The woman said to him, 'Sir, give me this water so that I won't get thirsty and have to keep coming here to draw water.' He told her, 'Go, call your husband and come back.' 'I have no husband,' she replied. Jesus said to her, 'You are right when you say you have no husband. The fact is, you have had five husbands, and the man you now have is not your husband. What you have just said is quite true.'

'Sir,' the woman said, 'I can see that you are a prophet. Our fathers worshipped on this mountain, but you Jews claim that the place where we must worship is in Jerusalem.' Jesus declared, 'Believe me, woman, a time is coming when you will worship the Father neither on this mountain nor in Jerusalem. You Samaritans worship what you do not know; we worship what we do know, for salvation is from the Jews. Yet a time is coming and has now come when the true worshippers will worship the Father in spirit and truth, for they are the kind of worshippers the Father seeks. God is spirit, and his worshippers must worship in spirit and in truth.'

The woman said, 'I know that Messiah' (called Christ) 'is coming. When he comes, he will explain everything to us.' Then Jesus declared, 'I who speak to you am he.'

John 4:13–26

A THIRST FOR GOD

There are two sorts of thirst. A physical thirst that longs for water and a spiritual thirst that longs for God. A longing for something—or someone—outside us to come inside us and quench our thirst. We feel more desperate when we are thirsty than when we are hungry.

As a child I suffered badly from bilious attacks, and, because of the advice of a misguided district nurse, my mother wouldn't allow me to drink anything while I was having an attack. The sickness was bad enough, but even worse was my desperate thirst. I used to imagine mountain streams with clear, sparkling water bubbling and tumbling over the rocks, and I would see in my mind fountains full of fizzy drinks. Miserable, I would suck the water out of my face flannel, and long to be better. Not just so that I wasn't sick any more, but so that I could quench my thirst.

The woman of Samaria had a thirst in her soul, and Jesus told her how she could quench it. He told other people, too. One day in Jerusalem he stood up in the temple and said in a loud voice:

'If anyone is thirsty, let him come to me and drink. Whoever believes in me, as the Scripture has said, streams of living water will flow from within him.' By this he meant the Spirit, whom those who believed in him were later to receive. Up to that time the Spirit had not been given, since Jesus had not yet been glorified.

John 7:37–39

Someone I know had a job abroad that was tough and fairly lonely. At times she became very tired and exhausted—and spiritually she felt very dry. Then she would kneel down by her bed and pray. 'Lord Jesus, I am thirsty,' she would tell him, 'so I'm coming to you to drink.' She would stay there on her knees, just being quiet and waiting. Then, after a little while, she would get up again and go back to work—and somehow

With You is the Well of life
In your Light we see light Ps. 36.9

her thirst had been quenched and she felt better.

When the disciples came back from their shopping expedition John says that they were surprised to find Jesus talking with a woman. But the woman is exhilarated. She goes back into the town and starts telling the people about Jesus.

> 'Come, see a man who told me everything I ever did. Could this be the Christ?' They came out of the town and made their way towards him. Meanwhile his disciples urged him, 'Rabbi, eat something.' But he said to them, 'I have food to eat that you know nothing about.' Then his disciples said to each other, 'Could someone have brought him food?' 'My food,' said Jesus, 'is to do the will of him who sent me and to finish his work.

> John 4:29–34

So we are back to eating and drinking—with ordinary water and ordinary food as symbols of a different sort of water and a different sort of food. A spiritual feeding on God—and drinking the water of the Spirit.

THE PRESENCE AND POWER OF THE SPIRIT

When Jesus taught his disciples about the Holy Spirit, just before he went up to Jerusalem to die, they found what he said very hard to understand. He was going away, and they didn't want him to go. He tells them that when he has gone he will come to them again, and although the world won't see him any more, they will. 'Why, Lord?' they ask.

> Jesus replied, 'If anyone loves me, he will obey my teaching. My Father will love him, and we

will come to him and make our home with him . . .
I tell you the truth: It is for your good that I am
going away. Unless I go away, the Counsellor will
not come to you; but if I go, I will send him to
you.'

John 14:23; 16:7

The Spirit is as invisible as the wind. But we can see the effects of the wind—and feel it. We can put up the sails in a little boat that is riding at anchor—and then as we get under way we feel the power of the wind as it fills the sails and takes our little boat fast across the water. No wind means no power—and no sailing.

It is like that with the Spirit. Invisible, mysterious, and powerful. Present in the hearts of all of us who believe in Jesus—but sometimes quenched and sometimes grieved. Then we are like a little boat with empty sails—not going anywhere, and not doing what our builder and maker created us for. People with no power to live the Christian life—and powerless to love other people.

But we don't have to remain powerless and helpless. The Spirit is still there, and there is a Helper and a Saviour. We can experience an inner renewal and the forgiveness of our sins. Fresh supplies are there for the asking and for the taking—and the way for us to make them our own is by feeding on God. We live out our Christian life day by day by doing just what we do at the start of it. We eat the flesh of the Son of man and we drink his blood.

FEEDING ON THE LIVING BREAD

So how do we do it? Jesus didn't tell us to do something difficult or impossible. It is as simple as eating and drinking—and the first great commandment shows us the way to it. Love is the way and love is the key.

> *'Love the Lord your God with all your heart and with all your soul and with all your mind and with all your strength.'*

Mark 12:30

Loving with all our heart. When we love someone we want to spend time with them. So we shall spend special times with God—when we go to church and when we pray and talk to him in a time of quiet every day. But we also know that his presence is with us during every moment of every day. We can't hold him at arm's length. He is still within us even if we try to distance ourselves from him—but then we are falling short in our loving, and our heart isn't feeding on him. Loving and being loved nourishes us like nothing else in the whole of creation—and the love of God for us is food that feeds our soul.

Our heart is the core of our being and the person that we are. You are you, unique in all the world, and I am I. Both of us created in the image and likeness of God—but both of us different. Just as every person in the world is different and unique. And each one of us can sing a unique and special song to the praise of the glory of God from the depth of our heart.

Loving with all our soul. Our soul is our true self—the new creation that is growing up into Christ. St Paul writes to the Galatians as 'My dear children, for whom I am again in the pains of childbirth until Christ is formed in you...' (Galatians 4:19). The image of a new birth runs all through the New Testament, and Peter encourages the new Christian to feed and to grow:

*Like newborn babies, crave pure spiritual milk, so
that by it you may grow up in your salvation, now
that you have tasted that the Lord is good.*

1 Peter 2:2–3

A baby grows best when it knows that it is loved—
and babies gurgle with delight when their mother looks
down at them with love shining out of her eyes. Love is a
food that nourishes all of us and makes us flourish—and
we can look into the face of God and know that we are
loved. And in deep satisfaction and happiness we
respond to his love by giving him ours. The beautiful
priestly blessing from the Old Testamnt is is about the
face of God:

'The Lord bless you
and keep you;
the Lord make his face shine upon you
and be gracious to you;
the Lord turn his face towards you
and give you peace.'

Numbers 6:24–26

The new life in us, which is our true self, feeds on the
love of God. And as we feed we grow up into love and
our love grows. Our love for God and for our neighbour
and also for ourself—because we become more and
more aware of our own enormous value and precious-
ness to God our Creator and redeemer, and also of the
fact that every human being in the whole world is just as
precious to God as we are, and just as greatly loved.

Loving with all our mind. Our minds are a vital part
of our loving, because it is through our minds that we

discover what real loving is and how to do it. After all his marvellous teaching about the Christian faith in the first eleven chapters of his letter to the Romans, St Paul urges his readers to:

> ... offer your bodies as living sacrifices,
> holy and pleasing to God—this is your
> spiritual act of worship. Do not conform
> any longer to the pattern of this world, but be
> transformed by the renewing of your mind.
> Then you will be able to test and approve
> what God's will is—his good, pleasing and
> perfect will.

Romans 12:1–2

Some of the information in our brain is incorrect—so we need to reprogram it, like a computer. Our brains are far more complex than any computer, but there is a similarity. And when we get the facts wrong we have to change them. The facts that we think are true about God might be wrong—and the way to correct them is to reflect on the life of Jesus, and to read the rest of the New Testament and most of the Old.

God has a passion for social justice—and when a nation oppresses the poor he is angry. If we don't believe that we have got it wrong. God is like Jesus—the friend of outcasts and sinners, and the servant king. God is a suffering God—and if we believe that he distances himself from our suffering and our pain then we have got it wrong again.

A few months ago in Britain a leading politician was calling for Christian ethics to be taught in schools. But the true facts are that Christian ethics flow out of a Christian life. Real loving is an inside job, not something that an anxious politician can impose on people because the country is falling apart at the seams through its lack of compassion and justice.

And absurdly, that same politician, who had been calling for Christian ethics to be taught in schools, was declaring publicly that the British government would not speak to the leaders of the IRA until the violence stopped. But the facts of Christian doctrine (which shape Christian ethics) tell us that God does far more than just speak to us when we are his enemies. In Christ, he died for us.

> You see, at just the right time, when we were still powerless, Christ died for the ungodly. Very rarely will anyone die for a righteous man, though for a good man someone might possibly dare to die. But God demonstrates his own love for us in this: While we were still sinners, Christ died for us. Since we have now been justified by his blood, how much more shall we be saved from God's wrath through him! For if, when we were God's enemies, we were reconciled to him through the death of his Son, how much more, having been reconciled, shall we be saved through his life!

> Romans 5:6–10

It might stick in our throats, but to feed our minds on Christian truth is to know that the God who is re-forming and re-making us in his own image—just like Jesus—is that sort of God. He is making us into people who love their enemies—just like Jesus.

We can tear up the Sermon on the Mount if we like, and stop printing it in our Bibles. But if we take it seriously it will transform us—and the hardest bit of all is Matthew 5:43–45.

'You have heard that it was said, "Love your neighbour and hate your enemy." But I tell you: Love your enemies and pray for those who persecute you, that you may be sons of your Father in heaven.'

In the Gospel of Luke, Jesus gave the same teaching in a slightly different and even tougher form:

'Love your enemies, do good to those who hate you, bless those who curse you, pray for those who ill-treat you.'

Luke 6:27–28

The only way we shall ever manage to do it is through the power of the Spirit of Christ within us and by praying—and to love God with all our mind is to find out what he wants us to do, and then to be transformed by the renewing of our mind.

Loving with all our strength. We shall need all our strength to pray in and then live out the radical manifesto that God has set out for us—and we shall have to do a lot of feeding on God to keep up our strength. The strength and the energy are available for us—and St Paul knew the mighty power of them in his own experience, and through the Christ within him. He wrote about it to the Colossians:

To [the saints] God chose to make known how great among the Gentiles are the riches of the glory of this mystery, which is Christ in you, the hope of glory. It is he whom we proclaim, warning everyone and teaching everyone in all wisdom, so that we may present everyone mature in Christ.

For this I toil and struggle with all the energy that he powerfully inspires within me.

Colossians 1:27–29 (NRSV)

BEING TRANSFORMED

The way of being transformed is the way of reflection—on the glory of God and on the facts about the nature of God as the word of God makes them known to us. We look at the life of Jesus in the Gospels—and we feed our souls and ourselves as his words and his actions enter into us and become a part of us. Then we become like him, and we enter into a new freedom of living and loving.

Now the Lord is the Spirit, and where the Spirit of the Lord is, there is freedom. And we, who with unveiled faces all reflect the Lord's glory, are being transformed into his likeness with ever-increasing glory, which comes from the Lord, who is the Spirit.

2 Corinthians 3:17–18

We are transformed into his likeness as we share in his nature—and when we do we are feeding on him, and letting ourselves be changed. 2 Peter 1:3–4 shows us the way of it:

His divine power has given us everything we need for life and godliness through our knowledge of him who called us by his own glory and goodness. Through these he has given us his very great and precious promises, so that through them you may participate in the divine nature and escape the corruption in the world caused by evil desires.

Believing the promises of God is one of the ways that we feed on him. Then our human nature participates in his divine nature—and the word participate means 'to possess something of the nature of a person, thing, or quality' (Webster). As we feed on God we start to possess something of his nature and qualities—and the glory of God will start to shine out of us like light in the darkness of his beloved world.

In our ordinary, human life, whatever we feed on becomes part of us. The incredible digestive processes of our body turn ordinary food and drink into us—into our eyes and mouth and hands and feet. The whole of our body is nourished and sustained in its life by the things that we feed on. But when we feed on God what happens is quite the opposite. The body and blood of Christ are not transformed into us. Instead, we are transformed into Christ.

On the night before he died, Jesus set up the sacrament that is right at the heart of the Christian faith.

REFLECTIONS FOR 'FEEDING ON GOD'

- Remember the last meal you ate, and what you ate. Remember where you were, and whom (if anyone) you were with. Let the taste of the food, and your surroundings, and the face of anyone else who was there, be present in your mind. Then, slowly and silently, read John 6:52–58 and spend some time just letting the words sink into you. Pray that Christ will show you more of how to feed on him and how to nourish your whole life with the life of God.

- In your imagination, see the events that John recounts in chapter 6 of his Gospel. Picture the enormous crowd of people who had come to listen to Jesus—with the Sea of Galilee—the blue of the sky

He has
filled the
hungry
with
good
things

Lk. 1.53

reflected in the water—and the hills in the background. Think about the people getting hungry, and about Jesus feeding the five thousand with the five small loaves and the two small fishes that the boy had put into his hands. Consider the concern of Jesus for the people's hunger—and think about their satisfaction when he fed them. Pray that he will satisfy you with himself—and teach you how to feed on him in your heart by faith.

• Read the words from the Psalms on page 55 about springs and rivers and the life of God, Read out the words of Thomas Traherne on the following page. Then imagine a river . . . and springs . . . and a sea . . . and reflect on the availablity of the life of God within you as you reflect on the pictures and the images. Pray that God will lead you into a deeper understanding of the wonder of the mystery of 'Christ in you, the hope of glory'.

• Think about my gooseberry fool that was past its sell-by date—and about some food of yours that went off and perhaps smelt horrible and crawled with maggots. Read John 6:44–51 on page 61. Then stay with the images and the words and pray in silence for a few minutes. Be thankful for the food that is God himself—the 'food that endures to eternal life'.

• Remember a time when you were very thirsty—and then remember the delight of quenching your thirst. Let that physical thirst make you aware of your spiritual thirst. Then remember the words of Jesus in the temple in Jerusalem, and turn them into your own prayer: ' "Let anyone who is thirsty come to me, and let the one who believes in me drink. As the scripture has said, 'Out of the believer's heart shall flow rivers of living water.' " Now he said this about

the Spirit, which believers in him were to receive . . .'
(John 7:37–39, NRSV).

- Have you ever experienced a drought? Perhaps a
major drought, when a whole country came close to
dying through lack of rain, and when plants and
trees, animals and human beings were virtually
without water. Or perhaps a plant that you had in a
pot wilted and drooped because you had forgotten to
water it. Think about water. The water that is vital
for physical life, and the water of life that flows out of
the heart of God into our hearts. Let those images put
you in touch with your own thirst and longing for
God (or perhaps with your absence of thirst). Then
ask Jesus to give you the Spirit of God, so that the
Spirit comes to you to quench your thirst. Or, if you
aren't thirsty, ask Jesus to give you a thirst for
himself.

- Imagine yourself in a little boat, becalmed on a lake.
There is no wind, so you cannot move. Then imagine
a wind starting to blow, and the sails billowing out
and taking your boat over the water. Ask yourself
where you want to go to in your life. What do you
think God is calling you to do with your life? Use this
hymn as a prayer:

O Breath of Life, come sweeping through us,
Revive your church with life and power.
O Breath of Life, come cleanse, renew us,
And fit your church to meet this hour.

O Wind of God, come, bend us, break us,
Till humbly we confess our need;
Then in your tenderness remake us,
Revive, restore; for this we plead.

O Breath of Love, come breathe within us,
Renewing thought and will and heart;
Come, love of Chirst, afresh to win us,
Revive your church in every part.

5

FEEDING ON THE EUCHARIST

It was Saturday evening, and Bill and Dolly had just got home from mass. They sat me down at their kitchen table while Bill started to peel some onions and courgettes in preparation for their supper. Dolly put their two new kittens out into the garden and went to get her missal. I was going to a party, but on the way there I wanted to find out from my Catholic friends what was the same and what was different about their service and mine.

When he had finished his peeling and chopping, Bill sat down with us at the table and we opened up our books—Dolly's white and gold missal and my green Alternative Service Book. As we went through them, paragraph by paragraph, we discovered how similar the services are. In some places the words are exactly the same.

All over the world—in one way or another—Christians do what Jesus told us to do on the night before he died. Whether it is a parish communion in the Church of England, a simple service in a house church, or a great papal mass in St Peter's in Rome, bread and wine are there at the heart of it. The body and blood of Christ given for us and to us—and the glory of that self-giving love shines like light into the darkness of our disunity and our differences.

When we had discovered how small the actual differences were between our two services, we shut our books and got out our diaries to fix a day for me to go to supper with them. We agreed on the following Saturday—and Bill asked me what sort of food I wanted to eat then. 'He's really into cooking at the moment!' said Dolly, who is a super cook herself and loves *his* cooking. 'You can have Indian, Chinese, or American...' Bill told me. 'What would you like?'

I thought for a moment—and then remembered the delicious salt cod and pasta served with thick slices of orange and a green salad that they cook for supper on Christmas Eve. So I opted for Italian—and in four days I shall be sitting at their table and eating with them. They will collect me on their way home from mass, and I shall book a taxi to take me home so that I can drink wine with the meal. Either Bill or Dolly will say grace before the meal—and because of our conversation last Saturday I shall inevitably be thinking about the eating and drinking at the heart of the sacrament that Jesus gave to us.

'This is my body,' Jesus had said at the Passover meal on the night before he died, and 'This is my blood.' The bread is the body and the wine is the blood. Broken bread that is the body of the Christ 'who bore our sins in his own body on the tree'. Wine that is the 'blood of the covenant, which is poured out for many for the forgiveness of sins'.

This is one of the two vital sacraments of the Christian faith. Baptism is the other. That happens to us just once in a lifetime. More often than not we are too small to remember it, but the fact, the benefits and the symbolism of it are there for ever.

When Martin Luther got depressed about the Church and about Christianity he would say to himself: 'I am baptized'—and in the remembering of the fact he would remind himself of all the promises of God that went with it. A new birth and a new life in Christ, with the promise and the gift of the Holy Spirit often symbolized sacramentally in the anointing with the oil of chrism.

The sacrament of baptism only needs to happen once, because once we have become members of the family of God we are sons and daughters for ever—even if we go away into the far country like the prodigal son. When we come home again we don't need to be baptized again. Just forgiven—and to run into the open arms of the Father who runs out to meet us.

But the sacrament of the eucharist, or holy communion, is a gift from God that we can be given Sunday after Sunday to nourish our life in Christ. As we eat the bread and drink the wine we are feeding on God in our heart by faith—and God-in-Christ crucified, and risen from the dead, is feeding us with himself.

Ever since the beginning, the Christian Church has done what her Lord told her to do in remembrance of him. The shape of the service is very much the same in all the traditions of the Church, and always, right at the heart of it, is a form of the words that Jesus spoke on the night before he died.

'Take, eat; This is my body which is given for you . . . Drink this, all of you; this is my blood of the new covenant, which is shed for you and for many for the forgiveness of sins.'

In any communion service, whatever form it takes, there are always certain things that happen (even in the Free Churches which have free prayer rather than a set liturgy).

• Some sort of preparation—to make people aware of the presence and the glory of God.

- Some form of confession followed by a declaration of the forgiveness of sins.

- Some listening to the historical truths of the Christian faith, through the reading of scripture and often a sermon. A telling of the Christian story through the ministry of the word.

- Some prayers for the Church, for the world and for ourselves.

- The eating of the consecrated bread and (in many churches though not all) the drinking of the consecrated wine: the body and blood of Christ. At that point in the service all Christians, according to the rites of their particular tradition, do what the Church of England service book tells Anglican communicants to do:

  Draw near with faith. Receive the body of our Lord Jesus Christ which he gave for you, and his blood which he shed for you.

  Eat and drink in remembrance that he died for you, and feed on him in your hearts by faith with thanksgiving.

I have been to communion in a Baptist chapel, and in that service we all went up to be given the bread to eat. Then we returned to our seats, and the deacons came round with trays and gave all of us our own tiny cup of wine. The symbolism of everyone drinking from one cup was missing—but we still experienced a real one-ness, because we didn't drink out of our own cup immediately. We waited—until each person had been served. Then we all drank together—and as we did we listened to the words being spoken to us, about the blood of Jesus being shed for for us, for the forgiveness of our sins.

After the eating and drinking, in all the churches, there is always more thankfulness in prayer for the greatness and glory of God's gift of himself to us. Then there is some form of final blessing and a sending out of the people of God into God's world—to be the light of the world in the power of the Holy Spirit.

The details are different. But the heart of the matter is the same. In any service we shall listen to the words, and eat the bread and drink the wine. And in all of it God will come to us and feed us with himself.

The Christians who come to it might call the service the breaking of bread, the mass, the eucharist, the Lord's supper, or holy communion. But whatever we call it—and in whatever way our understanding of it differs—the person who set up the sacrament on the first Maundy Thursday evening will be there with us. Loving us and teaching us and giving himself to us— just as he did to his disciples all the way through his life on earth when he had a human body like our own.

But for us it is far better than it was for them. He was outside them—but he is inside us. So the relationship is far more intimate, and it doesn't come to an end. When the disciples left the presence of Jesus, he wasn't with them any more. But we can't leave his presence—once he has come to dwell in us. And as it says in most of the forms of the service, and in the New Testament, 'we are the body of Christ'.

Yet the body of Christ needs to feed on Christ—and to remember his death and passion. Matthew, Mark and Luke tell us about the setting up of the sacrament in the upper room on the night before Jesus died. St Paul heard about it after the resurrection. He tells us what happened— and how we are to go on remembering what happened.

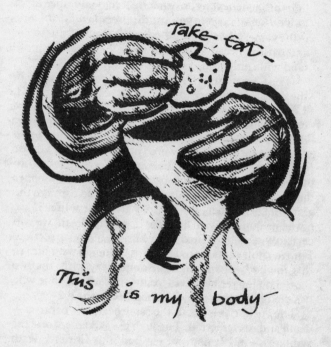

For I received from the Lord what I also passed on to you: The Lord Jesus, on the night he was betrayed, took bread, and when he had given thanks, he broke it and said, 'This is my body, which is for you; do this in remembrance of me.' In the same way, after supper he took the cup, saying, 'This cup is the new covenant in my blood; do this, whenever you drink it, in remembrance of me.' For whenever you eat this bread and drink this cup, you proclaim the Lord's death until he comes.

1 Corinthians 11:23–26

We feed on the Christ who died—so the death that he died becomes ours. 'We died to sin,' St Paul wrote to the Romans, 'how can we live in it any longer? Or don't you know that all of us who were baptised into his Christ Jesus were baptised into his death? We were therefore buried with him through baptism into death in order that, just as Christ was raised from the dead through the glory of the Father, we too may live a new life. If we have been united with him like this in his death, we will certainly also be united with him in his resurrection. For we know that our old self was crucified with him so that the body of sin might be done away with, that we should no longer be slaves to sin—because anyone who has died has been freed from sin' (Romans 6:2–7).

The eucharist is about the same events as baptism—death and resurrection. Through the sacrament and the symbolism of baptism we entered into Christ's death and resurrection—drowning and dying in the waters of baptism, and then coming out of them washed and alive with a new life. 'We *are* the body of Christ' we can say, and know that it is true. Then in the eucharist we feed on the bread and wine, the body and blood of Christ, and the Christ-life that is already ours is nourished by the life of the Christ who died and rose again from the dead.

At the eucharist we feed on God through things, through people and through words—in the same sort of way that we feed on God in the whole of our life. But in holy communion the feeding is concentrated and focused on the central act of the sacrament—the eating of the bread and the drinking of the wine.

The bread and the wine of the sacrament are an outward sign of an inner eating and drinking of the being of Christ—and through it God gives himself to us, and we feed on God.

A transformation takes place. Not the transformation which we make when we change earthly food into our human bodies. But a transformation which God makes, in which the spiritual food of the consecrated bread and wine transforms human beings into the body of the Christ who died for us. We *are* the body of Christ, but we need to be nourished and to feed the new life within us. And we feed on God, through Christ.

We feed on the Christ who died for us. But he didn't stay dead. God the Father raised him from the dead on the first Easter morning, and his disciples saw him and touched him. And in the Revelation to John on the isle of Patmos, the risen Christ says to him, 'Do not be afraid. I am the First and the Last. I am the Living One; I was dead, and behold I am alive for ever and ever!' (Revelation 1:17–18).

So at communion we share in the life of the one who died, but who is 'the Living One . . . alive for ever and ever'. Sharing and communion, and feeding on God, are happening all the time in the Christian life, because they are what the Christian life is. The drama of the communion service is the outward and visible sign of what is happening all the time—and it happens at the eucharist in a particular way and with particular power.

The eucharist is the sacrament in which the Church meets its Lord. We have communion with him, and we feed on him. We feed on him through things—as we reflect on all the things that we can see around us in church. The light streaming through the windows. The different colours of things. The walls. The communion table itself. The actions that are taking place there—and it is good to watch them and to be aware of them.

We feed on God through the words of the service, and through the Bible readings and the prayers. Taking them into ourselves and making them part of us—so that they can nourish us and build up our life in Christ.

We feed on God through the people all around us— remembering that we are the body of Christ.

We feed on God through the whole of the eucharist—and through the bread and the wine.

> *That we should 'take' and 'eat' is an indispensable aid which the sincere Christian cannot omit; but the one thing that matters is that we should 'feed upon him in our hearts.'*

> William Temple, *Readings in
> St John's Gospel*, Macmillan

> *'For my flesh is food indeed, and my blood is drink indeed. He who eats my flesh and drinks my blood abides in me, and I in him.'*

> John 6:55–56 (RSV)

- Before the service starts, either at home or sitting in church, take some deep breaths, and quieten yourself. Perhaps everything has been in a rush and you are feeling hassled. Whatever it is, it doesn't matter. You are coming to God just as you are—and that's how he wants you to come. I love a prayer poem which a friend introduced me to, and I often use the first two lines of it when I have managed to get myself into a muddle or a rush:

  Come as you are, that's how I love you.
  Come as you are, feel quite at home.

  So pray like that—in total confidence that you can come to Jesus just as you are.

- When you next go to holy communion, make a special point of being aware of how you are feeding on God through the things around you. Be aware of the building, and the chairs, and the light streaming through the windows—or the electric light enabling you to see in the darkness. You will be feeding on God in other ways as well—but be particularly aware of the things around you.

- The next time you go to communion do the same exercise, but being aware of how you are feeding on God through people.

- The next time be aware of how you are feeding on God through words.

- The next time gather all your previous weeks awareness and understanding together as you become more deeply aware of how you are feeding on God through the service itself.

*My spirit has become
dry because it forgets
to feed on you.*

Saint John of the Cross

If you have enjoyed reading *Feeding on God*, you may wish to know that BRF produce a regular series of Bible reading notes, *New Daylight*, which is published three times a year (in January, May and September) and contains printed Bible passages, brief comments and prayers. *New Daylight* is also available in a large print version.

Copies of *New Daylight* may be obtained from your local Christian bookshop or by subscription direct from BRF.

A FREE SAMPLE COPY of *New Daylight* containing two weeks of readings may be obtained by sending an A5 SAE marked 'New Daylight' to BRF.

For more information about *New Daylight* and the full range of BRF publications, write to: The Bible Reading Fellowship, Peter's Way, Sandy Lane West, OXFORD OX4 5HG (Tel. 01865 748227).